STRATEGIES FOR BUILDING A THRIVING ONLINE BUSINESS

STRATEGIES FOR BUILDING A THRIVING ONLINE BUSINESS

RWG PUBLISHING

RWG Publishing

CONTENTS

1	Introduction to Online Business	1
2	Market Research and Identifying Opportunities	4
3	Developing a Strong Business Plan	7
4	Creating an Effective Online Presence	9
5	E-commerce Platforms and Payment Gateways	11
6	Digital Marketing Strategies	14
7	Content Marketing and Social Media Engagement	17
8	Email Marketing and Customer Relationship Management	20
9	Analytics and Performance Tracking	23
10	Customer Service and Retention Strategies	25
11	Scaling and Growth Strategies	28
12	Global Expansion and International Markets	31
13	Risk Management and Cybersecurity	33
14	Legal and Regulatory Compliance	36
15	Funding and Financial Management	39

16	Case Studies of Successful Online Businesses	42
17	Conclusion and Future Trends	44

Copyright © 2024 by RWG Publishing

All rights reserved. No part of this book may be reproduced in any manner whatsoever without written permission except in the case of brief quotations embodied in critical articles and reviews.

First Printing, 2024

CHAPTER 1

Introduction to Online Business

Building and growing businesses online is no longer simply a matter of putting up a web page, adding a "shopping cart" and "checkout" facility (all of which might be part of a simple, common or garden "e-commerce site") and, "Hey-presto!" you are an electronic merchant. This may have been a recipe for quick and dirty money a decade or so ago, but today it will find most newcomers lamenting that "the site's not delivering... the web doesn't work...." They're right – too many are – but the causes, and the remedies, are often not well understood if they depend on any but the most recent experience of the business or its advisors.

Ferndale School, a small British educational establishment, established its first online presence in 1996. Since then, it has had the opportunity to learn alongside a wide variety of businesses ranging from traditional retailers, product designers, wholesalers and distributors of both manufactured and digital products to "consultancies," software developers, franchisors, and similar service organizations. Like them, we have learned at times through our own clients and, where possible, we have also studied more widespread market and site behavior. Some websites have been little more than expensive electronic postcards for their real-world parent businesses. Others have continued to be barely legitimate. Nonetheless, their profits all offer practical signs of what works and what does not, which are the foundations for practical action. That action is often in the nature of managing "content." We have been able to let many businesses profit from their own content and turn website management into a truly productive experience.

Definition and Scope of Online Business

Online business is the contribution of information technology in the development of various fields of business. One could define that with the creation of the internet, business has moved to that virtual world. The main benefit derived from using the internet, as the unique medium of business, is because of its virtual characteristic. The creation of websites as selling tools. We could not forget that the development of the business is not a static concept, but dynamic. That is why the development of different services that could lead the business to online has been important too. As we shall see, the development service based on the usable reports will be the real boost for the development of business-to-business relationships. Indeed, these relationships will be developed using these transactions, which will lead business operations to the internet hedges of the virtual world. The development of new operational framework, new solution providers, and the integration with back office software are the key factors of creation of new online ventures.

What customers experience when they visit an online business goes far beyond the technology used for the interface. Content, product organization, and arrival on this stage are all part of the total visitor experience of visiting an online business. Other customer contacts may include e-mail, telephone calls, and post delivery.

Customers receive information before deciding what to buy and after purchase as well. They can print information from the internet website, moving information via older information technologies of post, fax, and telephone. Online businesses can service customers with old technologies as the customer prefers. These online businesses have lower cost and often a service of better quality than conventional businesses. Their internet technology shows customers the same information and keeps the same communications as the older information technology.

Businesses increasingly use technology to conduct transactions and exchange information. These organizations' business is conducted largely or entirely over the internet. This type of e-business is an online business. As for any company, the primary purpose of an online business is its customers. An online business develops the information system to interface with customers for sales and service.

CHAPTER 2

Market Research and Identifying Opportunities

My point thus far is about strategy generally. However, there are many problems which are not currently specified. These are more difficult for SRP research, since as they are not known or identified, it is difficult to set up the environment. This is unfortunate, since it is not practical to set about solving every problem we face by the standard scientific process of trying to understand it so we can specify our standard models. Even when we are trying to solve more standard scientific problems, we recognize that it is rare that there exists only one theoretical tool which provides the solution. Even though trying to understand and specify a problem in standard symbols may lead to precise conclusions, we may have lost the insights which we had that pointed us to the general nature of the solution.

Care should be taken to allow the SRP to proceed at its own pace and not constrain it to those aspects which happen to have appropriate resources. It is essential to maintain a willingness to compromise, replacing the need to extract every last bit of knowledge from the data with rapid progress towards the solving of important, complex, real problems. In a true sense, investigation of real-world problems could be important in its own right as a guide to improving the approach to SRP development. I believe this level of compromise is essential for 'real-world' SRP. Although there are many projects with declared strategies, the imperative appears to be so strong that SRP sometimes ends as little more than an exercise in computing against stylized fact, rather than putting the emphasis on solving real problems.

Understanding Market Trends

The downside of this sort of situation is also worth noting. Because information can be accessed so easily and because customers specifically seek out what they want, many webs have very thin margins, needing to post a big enough return to make themselves viable commercial operations. They have existed on very little traffic with relatively little profit to keep them going. These sorts of sites are often bought up by larger sites, in effect achieving their positive returns with their exits. There are some barriers to entry in setting up a market-making site, which implies that it may always remain a modestly powerful business model.

The first and most important step to building any kind of business is to understand how the market works. For building an online business, you need not only to understand how real-world markets operate but also how the online environment compares and contrasts with the physical world. Online business is different in a variety of ways. The primary difference is in the customer reach. A product that can be sold only in a single area can now be sold all over the world. Even better, an online business can often scale very simply, limiting capital and labor resources. This can lead to a rapid rise in sales and profits. Instead of being a single solution for a single group, successful business web like many search engine or auction sites are now giant clearinghouses for all kinds of online commercial activity.

CHAPTER 3

Developing a Strong Business Plan

Writing a plan often results in some exciting discoveries about various aspects of your business, even if it is your second plan in a year. This will change with the business, the nature of the business, and the market demand. Your business will continually modify and update the model as needed. A business plan is never finished; it is always a work in progress. Use it as a guide and reference for each stage of your business development. Preparing your business plan will make you think and take a step back to reflect on important issues for your business. Most of your efforts within the business will be task-oriented. However, in order to be effective and to gain the most benefit, you have to spend time thinking, planning, and working "on" the business and not just "in" the business.

Developing a strong business plan before you start your online business is crucial, as online businesses often evolve and they can take on a life of their own. Frequently, a business that began by fulfilling a particular personal need expands into related or even unrelated areas. Consequently, efforts and resources can be scattered and become counterproductive. A well-structured business plan narrows the focus and outlines the process from understanding the initial business idea to the specific actions necessary to keep your plan evolving and up to date.

Key Components of a Business Plan

Starting a business is one of the most exciting and challenging undertakings that one can undertake. People must possess the motivation, expertise, and confidence to have a strong desire for the product or service that they are selling. By representing their product well on their website, they will give themselves the guardian and protector of their product and customers. Making a conscious decision requires making a consistent effort toward a long-term focus on the business. Think about the business, its location, and its current conditions. Then, describe the business. What is the concept behind the idea to start a business? Consider the long-term investment in the business and the continual investment in it. Recognize both strengths and areas for improvement. A business plan contains a powerful and long-term focus. Making a stretching and enriched description of the focus strengthens the plan and its vital purpose by representing the business person realistically.

Here's an insight into what is needed to develop a business plan. When we move ahead, we will be constructing a complete business plan. This plan will be based upon lengthy analysis discussed inside it. We will develop a business plan from an upfront description of the business and the long-term focus of the business. The projections contained in the plan will consider current conditions as well as become the focus of the business. The business will grow both personally and as a firm, bridging the ever-disappearing space between where we are now and where we will be in many years. It is an ongoing effort to establish and achieve a long-term direction.

CHAPTER 4

Creating an Effective Online Presence

Building an effective online presence means much more than just building an attractive website. Too many businesses rush into the creation of an online presence without fully understanding the basics. They spend a lot of time, energy, and money building a site that does not attract, retain, and sell to the visitors they have spent so much money attracting to your site. To get the most from your online business, you need to build an effective online presence. Building an effective online presence means much more than just building an attractive website. To achieve a good website, you must adhere to several strategies and avoid deprecated methods.

To get the most from your online business, you need to build an effective online presence. Building an effective online presence means much more than just building an attractive website. There are four main stages to building an effective online presence: understanding online marketing, building an effective online strategy, creating a relationship with your customers and understanding how to sell to them, and creating a website that attracts and retains long-term customers.

Website Development and Design

The development aspects presented in the following sections address behaviors necessary for the development of successful websites, their linking activities, promotion and distribution programs, opportunities for differentiated pricing strategies, and customer service issues. Finally, we conclude this section with a brief discussion of site evolution.

1. Use different website design activities to appeal to different customer segments. 2) Use email to collect customer opinions. 3) Use order tracking activities to find non-delighted customers. 4) Use promotions to cross sell and increase profit margins. 5) Use purchase order systems and discounts to appeal to business buyers. 6) Use web logs to monitor site usage. 7) Learn from other online stores.

Companies that begin an online sales initiative frequently underestimate the planning and attention required to assure a successful marketing effort. Successful virtual stores, catalogers, and B2B companies accomplish many of the same activities that their traditional counterparts undertake, including market research, product and service selection, pricing, promotion activities, distribution, and customer service. For instance, successful online stores "decorate" their websites to feature products, services, and specials intended to motivate consumers to explore their offerings. Organization and targeting of consumer segments are essential to successful site decoration. Retailers want to make shopping with them fun whereas wholesalers must focus on making website visits efficient for their business partners.

CHAPTER 5

E-commerce Platforms and Payment Gateways

The best platforms for online merchants provide a full range of services that help in building and growing business with drag and drop functionality, professional templates, and editors. Major platforms for building an online store include Shopify, Magento, and WooCommerce. Although the fundamental principles of design are all the same for an e-commerce site as any other, it is the response of the user that brings about the desired outcome. The interface is perhaps the most vital aspect of an online retail platform because it is at this 'end' where consumer and business meet. Combined with a strategic communications plan, expertise, product, and service are not totally transferred to the customer as consumption is not possible without the delivery of payment and receipt of goods. Shopify, Magento, Propay, Dwolla, and PayPal are reputable service providers.

It is important to understand the difference between an e-commerce platform and a payment gateway. An e-commerce platform meets the software needs that make it possible to manage an online storefront. Backend services such as inventory management, payment gateways, and hosting are essential to success. Payment gateways may be seen as a pillar of the e-commerce enabling infrastructure, as they are the technology that allows a website to accept payments. They can be provided by banks, payment service providers or processors, or specialized financial technology companies. Whether directly or indirectly, the gateway communicates between the buyer and seller's bank to authorize a charge and transfer funds.

Choosing the Right Platform

We launched our first website, a UK urban lifestyle store called DIGITAL EAST, in 2001. While the brand is no longer web-based, a few years of hard work built a strong little bridge to significant orders from Aim magazine's readers. Our second (successful) online store, Mish Mish, was launched before a single box of stock was sourced in a wholesaler's showroom, thanks to the speed of supplier acceptance and overwhelming customer enthusiasm. Setting up an online store became a necessary part of the preparation when Voco launched the label's international business in February 2003. Before we had a label stock in a collection, our expectations for growth had already widened. We sell more through online stores than business-to-business and wholesale distribution channels combined.

Anyone can set up an online shop on eBay, but it takes a little more effort and at least a few customer recommendations to build a store on Amazon, the world's largest online retailer. These mass marketplaces come with millions of weekly visitors, but they limit you in terms of store design and checks. By necessity, they have to be strict to weed out the worst of the scammers. With eBay, PayPal, and Amazon taking a percentage of sales, many successful online stores believe that it's time to invest in a more independent route to becoming a thriving online business. An independent store's management requirements are a step up in intensity, but when the sales, profits, and asset value swell, the rewards are well worth it.

CHAPTER 6

Digital Marketing Strategies

We can help increase your search engine rank with search engine optimization (SEO) techniques focused on creating and promoting high-quality content and adopting ethical and effective SEO strategies. By staying ahead of the curve and understanding the ever-changing world of search algorithms, we can help more of the people who want your products find your site on search engines like Google. Quality content is always a priority; it's designed not for search engine algorithms but for the real people you're trying to reach. Social media marketing is perfectly in tune with the social tech power of our digital age. We use social media marketing to attract attention to the actions you want your customers to take and create brand awareness with positive messages about your company. Attracting a like, comment, or share is the modern version of an old-fashioned word-of-mouth referral!

We use advertising and social media marketing to help you attract lots of people to your website. Digital ads can be annoying and intrusive, so our marketing experts work to make sure each ad is relevant and valuable for the person who sees it. When integrated with relevant social media marketing, your customers know they matter to you. Influencer marketing puts your company front and center with respected industry figures, who share the benefits of using your products with their sphere of influence. It's a direct endorsement of your brand that's worth its weight in gold. Email marketing is still the most cost-effective digital marketing tool. By personalizing and targeting newsletters to the right people through the right platform, you can turn casual site visitors into leads and nurture those leads into loyal customers. Small and medium size businesses like yours can achieve goal-oriented customer communications through the help of our email marketing experts.

Search Engine Optimization (SEO)

The real aim of this book is to help you grow your business quickly and without unnecessary cost, and that is best achieved by enabling you to do for yourself as much as possible. SEO is no exception to this rule. The process of creating and maintaining a good-quality site, with properly structured content (including a carefully chosen range of keywords), and organized metadata (detailed in section 7), optimized and web-compliant images and linking, plenty of regularly changing content and connecting traffic will take time initially but longer-term need not be onerous. Properly considered, effective SEO will even help improve your site and visitor experience overall. Good SEO practice is more a matter of getting to really know your audience well and anticipating their every need of you, your site, your content and the questions you are trying to answer. SEO has many moving parts, some of variable importance, depending on your target audience, content and business, but most such as those at its heart, are reasonably straightforward to understand and keep under your control.

Search engine optimization (SEO) is the art and science of driving traffic to your site from search engines by improving your site's organic search result visibility. Understanding the logic of how search engines like Google work is at the heart of good SEO. While there are many search engines, Google claims more than 60 percent of search engine traffic, so other search engine rankings are slightly less important than getting Google right. Google Search uses over 200 factors to determine where pages rank: these are closely guarded secrets, and the algorithm changes hundreds of times a year. However, understood well, there are several key strategies that will significantly improve your SEO. It must also be said that many agencies purport to specialize in optimization, with prices to match, and some services offer quite a good value, albeit in a limited sense. However, anyone can do a great deal of very effective SEO with solid training and no payment to outside experts.

CHAPTER 7

Content Marketing and Social Media Engagement

Always-online social media is everywhere — its presence can be felt and seen even from outer space. Getting noticed is the first step to getting connected. Keep in mind: the first conversations don't always have to be about business. It's still okay to say, "Hello. How can I help?" Take every chance to support and cheer. There are no shortages of examples where peer businesses in your chosen field — supporting, promoting, and sharing each other's posts — leave comments all the time on news and stories all around. It's important to do so as this level of commenting becomes part of your commenters.

We all strive to look for ways to get a step ahead of the game. Today, both social media engagement and that innovative "universal language" marketplace — always-online content — can both complement and supplement your every movement. Social Media – Empowering the Informed

Information Sharing: This information sharing is not only for customers, but – in sharing their posts – it also helps the businesses you are connecting with. All valuable information. However, it's important to stress that it can't be just a one-way street: this valuable information goes back and forth between all parties sharing on all sides. Creating content and talking it out with your audience.

Report: Building a loyal client list by offering well-timed help and follow-up communications is in everyone's best interest. Your social media pages — as part of an ongoing marketing effort — must offer a combination of posts, articles, alerts, status reports, infographics, expert Q&As, industry gossip and tidbits, inspirational quotes, and personal observation. Report online giveaways, as well as sharing pictures and videos to engage customers' attention.

Content Marketing – Making it Work for You Remember, people are interested in what they are interested in, and your information may or may not be of interest in a serious way. To compete in this space, always make sure that your research is not only up to the minute, but also reflects the changes in your chosen market. Listen to your clients and set yourself up to discuss the information they send your way. Ask questions and answer them with a blend of custom and self-created content.

Creating Engaging Content

I come to this area not only because the strategies for hooking visitors into your website have been capital to the successes of my own clients in my former career as an Internet services professional, but also because of my extensive background in applied psychology and performance technology. I can tell you that people can be enticed to do just about anything if you can find an opportunity for serving their needs strongly enough. For some, the easiest way to hold visitors will be by offering what they're looking for - better information or stronger motivation. For others into target for greater sales, a closer-to-right marketing strategy or a different configuration of the physical environment. However, the vast majority of the widely varying business website owners in position to benefit from the ways that visitortainment can be increased and how curiosity, anticipation, excitement, peripheral interest, and enticement can be piqued and proffered.

We'll look at credible research on the various factors, identify those that can be improved or added to a business website, and give you a roadmap that you can follow to do just that. Some of the changes that it is necessary to make aren't easy ones, but the payoffs can be huge. What's the difference between a dead, unproductive and wasteful and a thriving, busy and successful website? The answer is simply that the thriving website has what people are looking for. Don't get shortchanged by the prevailing wisdom that you can't make people change their ways. If you've got something they want, you can make people jump through hoops. The keys to what they want are two deceptively simple factors: bad enough problems and exciting enough interests.

CHAPTER 8

Email Marketing and Customer Relationship Management

You can ask for other ability verification, and offer additional comments to refer more people for incentives. Be sure to offer online support in your customer service autoresponders. Most companies require 30-60 days notice or a percentage of their future fees in order to implement this when you are setting it up or at a later time when your list has grown large. Also, cramming online support down a low volume support company's throat is probably going to be more of a hassle to the company with the large list, rather than effective strategies for both to share the setup charges and content. Use the fact that online support on common problems and complex installations is a real value add. They should respond favorably to at least a few basic autoresponders.

Offer an opt-out option immediately and on every follow-up message. This builds trust and makes your offer more comfortable and believable. It is also a way to qualify your lists because potential customers are carefully sifting through and deciding only to receive information that is important to them. This means if they are there, they are more likely to buy - from you. You would be wise to respect that. You can refine the process by setting up as many lists and follow-up series as your autoresponder program will allow. These can be sorted by demand for certain product groups, demographic data, or even major keyword submissions for groups of related web sites through search engine links. You can track potential customers by their "Where did you hear about us?" submission on your subscribe page so that you can learn which search engines or links are your best sources of leads, and which ones suck the profits out of the endeavor.

Building a Subscriber List

The first step into an email relationship is to acquire the right to communicate. To do this in ways that do not just get your missive spammed, mailed directly to trash, or generally resented, you must get the recipient or their mobile device owner's permission. Followers of Seth Godin's ideas on Permission Marketing will be well to the fore here. This is one of the big secrets to successful organic list building. Never, repeat never, buy in a list of SPAM addresses. Getting caught doing so can destroy your reputation as a netizen. Being seen to protect and respect the privacy of customers and clients speaks volumes about you and what your business stands for. Successful opt-in technologies are a key building block in permission marketing.

Any online business depends, at least partly, on the email conversations you have with clients, potential clients, and the merely curious. Many businesses rely on their regular broadcasts to clients and lists of prospective clients as their major marketing tool. It is a potentially highly effective way to build one-to-one relationships by bringing genuinely valuable content to the right people and encouraging feedback and interaction. Since the cost of sending emails instead of direct mail is virtually zero, the benefits to the business can be enormous.

CHAPTER 9

Analytics and Performance Tracking

Your website may be the cornerstone of your online presence, but it must be optimized with the needs of the user in mind. It is not enough to have a website that looks good. It must also work well. Just like a brick-and-mortar building needs to be well-maintained to stay looking nice, it is not enough for your website to look good when first built. It needs to be consistently maintained, modified, and updated to stay relevant, secure, and attractive. To simply put up a website with the intention of "working on it later" is a pointless, costly exercise. You have to have a functioning website if you ever want to have a chance of being successful in the world of online business.

While most people see the value in an online business, many people don't realize the ways they can help enhance and grow their business. The point is that having a website isn't enough on its own for a business to thrive. It takes commitment, strategy, and an investment of time and capital to create a successful online presence.

Here are strategies that can help make your online business a long-term success.

Key Metrics for Online Businesses

You really do not have to wait until all of your reports are ready before you begin your analysis and find trends and hotspots. To be doubly sure, do a casual review of your lists for troubling trends, with a focus on those metrics that could cause immediate distress and require your intervention. For instance, are the orders, sales, and conversion rates adequate to feed the activities of the rest of your business? Keep in mind that a growing list without corresponding and growing orders and sales is like a stomach that can hold more food but never gets any food! Is the customer retention rate adequate to ensure that your business will be around for the long term?

A popular adage in the financial world says "Strike while the iron is hot." Using this adage, you must first identify those iron-hot metrics that best help you to manage your business every month. Then you must review favorable trends every month to ensure that you are indeed continually working to make your business sizzle. When the iron is indeed hot, each month you should make that incisive strike and identify at least one action item that can be immediately applied to your business to bolster the favorable trend. A well-placed and timely action item can help you grow your business more, increase sales, increase your response rate, improve your conversion rate, improve your average order size, increase your retention rate, increase frequency of visits, reactivate forgotten customers, and increase the lifetime value of your customers. In addition, the timing of this action can generate greater results without necessarily having to spend more money.

CHAPTER 10

Customer Service and Retention Strategies

Why do businesses adopt customer service and retention strategies? The odds of selling to an existing customer are 1 in 2, as compared to the odds of selling to a new customer, which are 1 in 10. Existing customers have shown that they trust your business enough to spend money with you. Many businesses take for granted that an individual has made a purchase from them and therefore did make the right decision when choosing their product (in most cases, the decision to purchase has been made). Businesses with this mindset neglect their core customers and overspend on marketing gimmicks to attract new customers, instead of reaping the benefits of having a business that is known for its excellent relationships with its customers. Smart business owners use their knowledge of the purchasing cycle to their advantage, seeking new ways to extend their relationship with existing customers.

What are customer service and retention strategies? Customer service is the process of interacting with your customers on behalf of your business. Popular strategies for customer service include providing information about a product or service, solving problems with a product or service, providing product-related updates, and taking the customer's payment. The customer service and retention strategies discussed in this chapter focus on how to serve and keep customers who have already purchased from you in the past. These individuals already know and trust your business, so designing customer service and retention strategies to keep them happy can be both easy and profitable.

Importance of Customer Feedback

Companies are often scheduling both public and private performance dates months in advance and need to anticipate final box office sales months in advance. Consequently, they must have up-to-date information in order to focus on long-lead media, which may often take as much as six months to book concerts, theater, and playbills. Furthermore, public performances are designed to generate consumer interest in all of the other products, such as the exchange tickets, movie TV special sales, compact disk sales, and souvenirs, which customers have shown a clear interest in. Additionally, an artist will want to know who is responding to flyers in the street boxes. Once the customer feedback mechanism is understood, the company can take steps to leverage it by integrating the feedback into the strategic decision-making process through tactics for tracking and leveraging customer interactions.

It has been said that a business is only as good as its team. Therefore, customer feedback is critical. The most reliable information available to a business usually comes from its employees or sales force, who know client perceptions. They are usually in touch with clients and know what they want and how they feel about the products and services being offered to them. Yet, most customer feedback mechanisms are inefficient, costly, inaccurate, and slow to use. To understand why this is so, we must study the most common ways that businesses try to evaluate customer feedback. The main sources of feedback include such methods as comment cards, customer hotlines, surveys, verbal interviews, and outside consultants. All of these mechanisms suffer from various degrees of slowness, inaccuracy, and outdatedness.

CHAPTER 11

Scaling and Growth Strategies

Growth is the desired target of practically every new and established company. It is, however, not the only metric that investors want to see. They also want to see proof of scalability in the business engine as customers' needs and behaviors change along their journey. Furthermore, scaling may be painful and involved and on its own not deliver the desired results. Achieving high profitability can be just as important as growth rates. Many companies have achieved scale but are finding it hard to achieve success and longevity. In this section, we describe a number of strategies and concepts that will help sustain high growth and revenue while optimizing the business for optimal profitability.

As customers' needs and behavior change along their journey, it is important for your business to adapt and adjust to these changes. This part of the book delivers strategies to grow and scale. These include understanding the drivers of your ultimate scalable growth engine to achieve rapid and profitable growth, finding a way to access high-quality customer interest, creating an effective and efficient way to turn this customer interest into revenue, delivering on the brand promise by creating an outstanding, high-value user experience that resolves customer needs, providing an environment that fosters and enables growth and change while maintaining the scalability and efficiency of the overall operational footprint, and ensuring that you have a high-profit engine to ensure that as your revenues grow, your company becomes increasingly profitable and more rapidly cash-flow positive.

Expanding Product Lines

It may be possible to cost-effectively distribute a broad mix of products to a local or niche market in the future. Cryptography and digital delivery mechanisms will need to be much improved. Product/sales fulfillment systems will require less attention than they do today if e-retailers are to switch from providing a narrow range to a full line of products. Business-to-business e-business suppliers are more likely to operate from catalogs first and foremost due to product awareness and associated sales costs. E-businesses are better at providing vast choices of products or product varieties than their conventional retail counterparts if goods make sense. Offerings of pure information. The invention and dissemination of information products are low cost and often automated. Original components are not difficult to produce, making it possible to provide information products for a large number of topics.

Full line coverage is one of four strategies you could pursue to increase sales, broaden customer reach, and deepen customer loyalty. Combining the above strategies will further fuel the growth of your incredible e-business and keep competitors at bay. As suggested earlier, you might decide to act on particular strategies and ideas in stages while shifting to full-line coverage can't be made complicated by customers taking it badly. E-businesses generally find it easier to move in this direction, providing a broad mix of product types.

If your initial affinity group contains people outside of your geographic catchment area or you and your market are willing to put up with the old with respect to delivery time, you will be able to satisfy a diverse affinity group with a broad mix of products.

CHAPTER 12

Global Expansion and International Markets

So, you've made it in your home market. Your online store is bustling with customers, and your appeal continues to grow. The store's income can be charted on an upward climb, and you've been looking at opportunities for expansion. There's still much to be done in your domestic market to capture the greatest possible percentage of your potential market with satisfying growth in the income store. But you don't have to stop there. The World Wide Web and Internet are redefining business, giving you the platform to easily sell your products and services internationally. As your business has grown and attained its share of the domestic market, you're probably well positioned to launch a global evolution. You need to have a long-term viewpoint, especially when it comes to positioning your online business estate as a global merchant.

You've established an online business and you're finding success in your home market. With the goods and services you sell, have you considered expanding globally? The Internet is the world's largest marketplace, which means your doorstep is open to international sales. Why swim in a pond when you can frolic in the ocean? It is easier now than ever before to open your online business's doors to the international stage. But it is not difficult to be misled by promising, yet unrealistic, international opportunities that result in lost time and wasted effort. This chapter discusses the reasons to enter the international market, the main ingredients of successful global evolution, and finally some considerations to keep in mind should you decide to take the plunge into international selling.

Adapting to Cultural Differences

Without question, legal and operational constraints must be taken into account for each and every host country. Multinationals are quite aware of these and attend to these specifics to operate within the mandates that are available. Small and medium-sized companies that identify cultural differences and adapt their products to these differences can brand themselves at an additional level. At the height of culture, and not counting religious or historical differences, food consumption presents a difficulty. The table is a privileged area of cultural expression. In particular, rejection related to foods was found across cultures. Bananas are placed, but not corn on the cob. For speed, both hands are used to express perseverance, but your neighbor will not be helped.

Cultural differences are seen between countries or regions within a specific country. We are referring to subcultures: old Europeans, new Asian Tigers, and third world. When catering to capital transfer transactions to diverse parts of the world, focus is on specific areas: transaction financing, long-term management assistance, and the home country control ratio. With respect to transaction servicing, focus must center on logistical support to guarantee optimal product sales, goodwill (testing host country markets for suitability, for instance), and product adaptation to cultural specificities.

CHAPTER 13

Risk Management and Cybersecurity

A hacker generally denotes a person with a high level of technical competence, especially with respect to decomposing and undermining software, including internet security measures. The term "hacker" was originally a nickname directed at people who built computers and software at MIT in the 1950s and through the 60s. Older generation computer users and students at MIT remember the better days of hackerdom, the 1970s, as those of technophiles who "hacked" hardware and software to make it perform in unexpected ways. Although knowledge of computer hacking and some virus writing, or the use of these tactics against anyone without consent is illegal, the technology skills can be very good indeed and are marketable, as shown by commercial security counter companies. In contrast to hackers, crackers are people who break into computer systems with abusive intent. They are also seen as wanting to damage high security military and commercial systems, they use technical knowledge in breaking copies of copyrighted software. The term is getting older and is rarely heard.

In a connected world of global communications via the internet, the risks of attack on your business are great. Everyday businesses are challenged by the tremendous financial and strategic challenges resulting from unprepared and/or outdated security environments that cost them money year after year. The threat of cybersecurity continues to dominate the public discussion of security concerns given its potential for damage to individuals, institutions, and nations. This material reviews cyber threats and network security fundamentals in the unique context of ES business. Possible incentives for investment in improved network security are reviewed, and some popular technologies suggested as "silver bullet" solutions to network security are introduced.

Protecting Customer Data

Protecting your business - a ten-point plan: • Secure Your Customer Database • Protect Your Website • Security Compliance Certificates • Payment Card Industry Data Security Standard (PCI DSS) • Privacy Policy and Security Certificates • Choose a Trusted Hosting Service for Your Website • Protect Your Regular Business • Protect Your Intellectual Property • Use an 'Electronic Store' Software Package • Don't Keep Information on Your Customers

The increase in internet fraud, customers' fears of identity theft and advance fee fraud means that you have to 'prove' to your customers that your business is not fraudulent, either through your website design or marketing methods. Moreover, without the existence and backing of a third-party customer complaint policy or a customer satisfaction guarantee, why should a customer trust you or your product? They are simply going to find it harder to trust you or your product and it will have an adverse effect on your order rates.

There are lots of things to think about when you're crafting a business plan for an online business. In many ways, building an online business is a bit like building a conventional bricks and mortar store. However, in some ways, building and running an online business is a bit easier, as technology takes care of some of the tasks which would consume longer periods of your time in a physical store. However, today's technology also throws up challenges which retail businesses of the past probably didn't have to think about at all and, if they did, these were much lower-priority issues.

CHAPTER 14

Legal and Regulatory Compliance

P.S. Several businesses provide services to help entrepreneurs who want to form a corporation or LLC. Their services are not expensive. They help ensure that what you file with the secretary of state, including your articles of incorporation or organization, have the kind of terms that will provide the protections and benefits that you desire. After forming your corporation or LLC, comply with your state's annual reporting requirements. They usually involve filing an annual report with the secretary of state and paying any applicable fee. Small, proprietor-owned firms often select being a limited liability company until an operational milestone is achieved. After that, they become a general corporation.

There are specific business entity models that owners of online businesses should consider. You can form a partnership, a corporation, a limited partnership, a trust, a cooperative or an exclusive purpose entity. To protect personal assets, most owners select either the general corporation or the limited liability company and receive personal liability protection. If the business disintegrates, these owners' personal assets are safeguarded (except where personal guarantees or transactions between the owners and the business could change that protection). The most popular choice today is the limited liability company, or LLC, which often provides the best of all worlds. Check with a business attorney to get advice on the best entity for you.

Offering digital products often qualifies you as an e-commerce business. For that reason, you need to be very particular about how you form your business entity, the kind of liability insurance you purchase, the notice you provide to third parties, your rights and responsibilities when you gain access to and store customer financial and other confidential information, entering into contracts with all owners and more.

GDPR and Data Privacy Regulations

Now, though it is essential, entrepreneurs should only become aware of this once they are deeper in their learning journey. The real challenge is to connect and make them aware early in the journey, and to teach effective strategies for both enriching others and themselves while creating a successful business. These aspects of entrepreneurship regarding fundamental value generation are not only noble but also typical for European business culture. By looking at the content of GDPR, we should be able to help EU entrepreneurs create businesses that operate with an understanding of user privacy and consent, and respecting user rights. We should also let EU entrepreneurs know that building and operating with such understanding does not negatively impact business prospects; on the contrary, it can positively impact sales and business success.

Every entrepreneur hopes that the company they are building will do well. Not only that they will be able to create a successful product or service and achieve profitability, but also ideally enrich both the people working with and the one using their offering.

Helping individuals, providing jobs, and creating shareholder value are very laudable goals. Business is not a sport and making money, and anyone who teaches startups should always remember that these are not mutually exclusive goals. You are better off teaching new entrepreneurs the importance of maximizing the pie for everyone.

Because the internet is a borderless environment that connects devices with servers within seconds, often crossing a multitude of international boundaries during a single session, to address the privacy concerns and harsh realities like the use of browser and device fingerprinting, no consent requirement for so-called purely first-party HTTP cookies, or the fact that relying on the implementation of proper deletion of tracking data conflicts with cases in which it would break websites or make them run slower, have led to further refinement of user protection based on understanding the open operation of the web. To have a deeper understanding should help early entrepreneurs build respectful and ethical businesses. There are more things, especially with the General Data Protection Regulation (GDPR), that are going on in the world of privacy, user rights, and ethics.

CHAPTER 15

Funding and Financial Management

The key to doing this successfully is finding a way to live on less money than you are making. This is difficult in the beginning, however, when your personal income is lower, it is important to develop the habit of savings early in your business's growth stage. Wise entrepreneurs will continue to set aside 20 percent of their profits regardless of the business's economic position. Doing so will grow the business's cash reserves and help to expand the business through the good times and help it to sustain growth through the lean times. Start saving today and your business will be better prepared to move towards the financial security you deserve.

Having an ongoing financial plan for your business is something that cannot be overemphasized. Many businesses fail not because they have poor products or services, but because they lack long-term financial plans. Building ongoing cash reserves for your business is an excellent way to get started. Many entrepreneurs who begin businesses today make the mistake of using all the business profit for personal use, while other businesses spend all the profits and find themselves short of cash when major expenditures are warranted. One excellent strategy is to set aside 20 percent of the business's profits every month in a separate savings account.

Bootstrapping vs. Seeking Investors

In any case, you should use your own funds or operating capital upfront to create the prototype for your online service, your go-to-market strategy, and most importantly, your customer-driven business model. If you are not prepared to put your own capital at risk, why should any outside investor be interested? In other words, to get capital, you need to show people that you have what it takes to bootstrap and get a real business going. And if the project is not worth it to you to bootstrap, then there would be no point at all in asking an outsider to finance it. With only a few notable exceptions, you should first put your own money into the business and drive your new venture to a working and cash-generating model using competent operating cash. Only then should you bring aboard an investor, be it an angel, a venture capitalist, a strategic investor, or a combination. With a working model in place that is generating revenue, you will have made your business incredibly more attractive to potential investors. Now you have a company that has gotten more attractive.

Many online businesses are at a disadvantage due to inconsistent cash flow, at least until the ads have been placed, the links exchanged, and the first revenues have come in. During this bootstrapping phase, it's the determination, ambition, and creativity of the developer that pay dividends beyond the cash investment in the business. Some of the most successful online entrepreneurs have done it largely on their own and shun rather than seek external investment. We're not knocking investors, mind you. New funding from angels or VCs can be vital at various stages of building your company. Bootstrap to the point where you have a prototype of your creation and an understanding of your target audience. You can then find an investor who can provide both the cash and the experience as well as connections or business partnerships to help you expand.

CHAPTER 16

Case Studies of Successful Online Businesses

There are many roads to the creation of a successful online business. There may not be one sure route to success, but in many cases, there is a pattern. This chapter presents thirteen actual case studies of the first stages of successful online business development. Each case has its own unique twists and turns, yet they share the common goal of generating sales and customers. In each of the case studies, you will discover conceptual ideas that you can apply to your own online business development. A case study might provide you with the underlying idea to identify the business opportunity in the first place. It may provide you a model that you can follow regarding how to best maximize sales or how to keep your costs low.

Learning from the successes of others can be a very effective way of shortening your own learning curve. In this case, you have the advantage of learning about successful online businesses in the context of the strategies of online business success. Keep the lesson in mind as you read each case study. How did the business make money? If they didn't, what strategies were they employing to increase sales or to earn a commission? What did they do to attract visitors to their site? Once there, how did they keep people on the site to make sales? What did they do to move people up through the buying process? Use the answers to these questions to help guide you in the building of your own online business.

Lessons Learned from Industry Leaders

Bringing together thought leaders to highlight diverse directions and strategies is a route to making a business contribution that will be needed now and tomorrow. These individuals have worked on the leading edge of the information society that includes free information, commercial interests providing for-profit services, databases of knowledge, tools using XML and intelligent algorithms, and more. Their experience represents groundbreaking technological solutions. Their insights on the most important skills necessary for succeeding in business highlight ways you and your contributions can make a difference not just for an individual venture but also for the success of the overall business venture, industry, and Internet.

Ongoing success in e-commerce can be a complex and subtle process. To help stimulate your thoughts on the most important ingredients, let's look at some perspectives on building a thriving business from the leaders in various e-commerce industries. The power of discussion in helping newcomers define what they should be concerned with, and what direction would be most useful, could not be better demonstrated than with the unique insight of the 23 leaders who provided these success lessons in e-tailing, e-marketing, publishing, content, advertising, software tools, services, financial services, search, auctions, and community development. Their "lessons learned" can and should be related to the type of companies and services you can contribute toward so that you are at the cutting edge of the next defining technologies in business development.

CHAPTER 17

Conclusion and Future Trends

Current internet use and exponential growth trends leave few observers surprised about how it quickly became the Information Superhighway. However, the ease of web use and the vanished geographical barriers for end-users have enticed more and more users, demanding more and more resources from the web environment. During the last few years, electronic commerce has been undeniably increasing, and records of breakthrough sales on the web are continuous. As a consequence, people whose business lies in the real world are looking for the business opportunities in the electronic dimension, intrigued by both the attractiveness of online sales and the potential for new market niches. After all, the web is open for business 24 hours a day, 365 days a year, with worldwide reach at a low cost.

Nowadays, the internet has become a part of the majority of people's daily life. Online business has been growing rapidly for over a decade. This book discusses the strategies for building a thriving online business from a practical point of view. The book has provided the guidelines, strategies, and key factors that are crucial for creating a successful online business. These key factors can be used as a guide for establishing a viable online business front end. The guidelines and strategies provided by this book begin by defining a winning idea for an online business. Then, the book addresses the important elements of developing an effective business plan for products and our website. How to market our products online, creating win-win relationships with our suppliers, and managing our website is also thoroughly discussed.

Emerging Technologies in E-commerce

As with most web-based programs, cost is coming down. Recently, some ASP vendors have started offering ASP savings similar to what small businesses could achieve by buying their own merchant services.

Some of our favorite e-commerce models are sites that market items provided by others. This is a high-profit but low-risk model that is excellent for solo entrepreneurs. Some of the best-known firms that use this model are Amazon.com and eBay. In fact, eBay provides a very low-risk way of determining if your product is saleable.

Another company using web-based software is 3M, which is using the InterWorld system to deliver hundreds of thousands of products to its business audiences, which consist of librarians in search of information, schoolteachers for A-V products, and parents in search of educational toys. This company is also planning to offer business services such as office supplies and consumer goods like DVDs.

By the time people feel comfortable with the current generation of e-commerce software, a new generation is being developed. One trend in e-commerce is the dramatic growth of software for businesses that provide subscription services. When businesses do this, customer information has to be secure and easy to use. Ideally, customers should be able to change their addresses and credit card information themselves without requiring customer support. This has led to the development of tools like E-Online's Storefront Service which handles all of the information for an e-commerce site.

Milton Keynes UK
Ingram Content Group UK Ltd.
UKHW040938081224
452111UK00011B/230